W9-DFF-414

LIBRARY CHARGES
FOR MISSING CARD

E 599   27,301
F   Fowler, Allan

            Please don't feed the bears

          SUGAR GROVE PUBLIC LIBRARY DISTRICT
             54 Snow Street / P.O. Box 231
                Sugar Grove, IL 60554

Rookie Read-About™ Science

DISCARDED

Please Don't Feed the Bears

By Allan Fowler

Images supplied by VALAN Photos

Consultants:
Robert L. Hillerich, Ph.D., Bowling Green
State University, Bowling Green, Ohio

Mary Nalbandian, Director of Science,
Chicago Public Schools, Chicago, Illinois

Fay Robinson, Child Development Specialist

SUGAR GROVE PUBLIC LIBRARY DISTRICT
54 Snow Street / P.O. Box 231
Sugar Grove, IL 60554

ℂℙ CHILDRENS PRESS®
CHICAGO

Series cover and interior design by Sara Shelton

Library of Congress Cataloging-in-Publication Data

Fowler, Allan.
    Please don't feed the bears / by Allan Fowler.
      p. cm. — (Rookie read-about science)
    Summary: A simple introduction to the physical characteristics,
habits, and natural environment of bears.
    ISBN 0-516-04916-X
    1. Bears—Juvenile literature. [1. Bears.] I. Title.
  II. Series: Fowler, Allan. Rookie read-about science.
QL737.C27F68 1991
599.74'446—dc20   91-3130
                                                    CIP
                                                    AC

Copyright © 1991 by Childrens Press®, Inc.
All rights reserved. Published simultaneously in Canada.
Printed in the United States of America.
1 2 3 4 5 6 7 8 9 10 R 99 98 97 96 95 94 93 92 91

Where do you find bears ?

Most of them live in the
woods.

6

A bear family's home,
or den, might be a cave

or a snow den,

or a hollow tree.

Bears love to eat.

That's why people say,
"I'm as hungry as a bear!"

Bears eat fruits and berries and other plants.

They eat small animals and
insects.

Some bears can snatch fish out of a stream with their paws.

Many bears spend the winter sleeping inside their dens.

Bear cubs are born in the winter.

When spring comes, the
cubs finally leave the den
and enjoy playing in the
woods outside.

The bears you see most often are called black bears.

The biggest bears are the
ones called brown bears.

A grizzly is a kind of
brown bear.

22

Polar bears are white.

They live in the Arctic,
the land close to the
North Pole.

Their thick coats keep them warm when they swim in the icy waters.

Bears look funny when they stand on their hind legs, and when they do tricks in the circus.

But they are really wild animals.

So please don't ever, ever feed a bear—not in the zoo, not in the woods.

You could get hurt.

And the bear has enough to eat anyhow!

Words You Know

bears

black bears

brown bears

cubs

grizzly bears

polar bears

dens

cave

hollow tree

snow den

The Arctic

Index

About the Author

Allan Fowler is a free-lance writer with a background in advertising. Born in New York, he lives in Chicago now and enjoys traveling.

Photo Credits

Valan—© Murray O'Neill, Cover, 17, 18, 30 (top left and center); © Aubrey Lang, 3, 15, 19, 30 (top right); © Wayne Lankinen, 4, 7, 14, 16, 27; © Stephen J. Krasemann, 5, 11, 21, 28, 30 (bottom left); © Hälle Flygare, 6, 31 (top left); © Fred Bruemmer, 8, 22, 24, 30 (bottom right), 31 (center and bottom); © R. D. Stevens, 9, 31 (top right); © Dennis W. Schmidt, 12; © Bob Gurr, 13; © Jeff Foott, 20
COVER: Black Bear